# College Planning
## for
## High School
## Students

### A Quick Guide

D0921308

# College Planning
## for
# High School
## Students

## A Quick Guide

M Y C H A L   W Y N N

COLLEGE PLANNING FOR HIGH SCHOOL STUDENTS: A QUICK GUIDE

ISBN 13: 978-1-880463-68-0
ISBN 10: 1-880463-68-7
Copyright © 2007 Mychal Wynn
Copyright © 2007 Rising Sun Publishing, Inc.
First Edition
Printing    1

The material contained in this book has been taken from the book, *A High School Plan for Students with College-Bound Dreams* covered under U.S. copyright by the author and publisher. All rights reserved. Any reproduction of material covered in this book without the expressed written permission from Rising Sun Publishing, Inc., is strictly prohibited except when quoted in brief reviews. No part of this book may be reproduced or transmitted in any form or by any means, electronic or mechanical, including photocopying, recording or storing in any information storage and retrieval system for commercial purposes.

Cover design and student photographs by Mychal Wynn.

Reference sources for style and usage: *The New York Public Library Writer's Guide to Style and Usage* copyright 1994 by The New York Public Library and the Stonesong Press, Inc., and the *APA Stylebook 2004* by the Associated Press.

Rising Sun Publishing, Inc.
P.O. Box 70906
Marietta, GA 30007-0906
770.518.0369/800.524.2813
FAX 770.587.0862
E-mail: info@rspublishing.com
Web site: http://www.rspublishing.com

Printed in the United States of America.

# Acknowledgments

I would like to thank those parents, educators, counselors, and mentors who have embraced the strategies outlined in the book, *A High School Plan for Students with College-Bound Dreams*, upon which this book is based, and who are working diligently to help more students pursue their college-bound dreams.

# Dedication

To my wife, for her patience, understanding, and support; our sons, Mychal-David and Jalani; the thousands of students and parents I meet each year who have college-bound hopes and aspirations; and to those who sacrifice each day on behalf of students and their dreams.

# Table of Contents

# About the Author

Mychal Wynn was an unlikely college-bound student, having been expelled from Chicago's De La Salle Catholic High School and barely earning enough credits to graduate from Chicago's Du Sable High School. Even more miraculous was his being accepted into Northeastern University, at that time, the largest private university in the United States and the only college to which he applied. Without a mentor to advise him or the benefit of the type of college planning outlined in this book, he had not taken the required courses to be admitted directly from high school into college. He received a *conditional acceptance*—conditional upon his taking and passing classes in Physics and Calculus (courses which were not offered at his high school). As a result of his not having the opportunity to take the necessary classes in high school, his college dreams were deferred as he was required to enroll in Chicago's Kennedy-King Junior College for one semester in the fall of 1974. While working the night shift at the U.S. Post Office from 10:30 p.m. until 2:30

a.m., he took classes in Physics and Calculus during the day, receiving an 'A' in Physics and a 'B' in Calculus.

In January 1975, he boarded his first airplane as he flew from Chicago, Illinois to Boston, Massachusetts, where he entered into the Northeastern University College of Engineering. In June 1979, Mychal Wynn became his family's first college graduate, receiving his Bachelor of Science degree. This once unlikely college-bound student was a highly recruited college graduate and has worked for such multinational companies as IBM and the Transamerica Corporation. In 1985, he and his wife, Nina, founded Rising Sun Publishing, where his wife serves as the Publisher and Chief Executive Officer and he serves as the principal trainer and Chief Financial Officer.

Mr. Wynn, his wife, Nina, and their two sons, Mychal-David (currently attending Amherst College), and Jalani (currently attending middle school), reside in Georgia.

# Introduction

Many students find themselves scrambling as high school juniors or seniors to take the SAT or ACT, identify the colleges that they are interested in applying to or the colleges that they believe that they can get into, while parents scramble to find the money to pay for the high cost of college tuition, room, and board. To avoid finding yourself in such a situation, this book, together with the book, *College Planning for Middle School Students*, is designed to provide you with a commonsense, comprehensive college-bound plan.

This book provides a quick guide to the information contained in the book, *A High School Plan for Students with College-Bound Dreams [Wynn, 2005]*. Due to space limitations, strategies will generally contain brief descriptions and, subsequently, will require more extensive reading or research on the part of the reader. Please refer to the *book* and *workbook* for more extensive reading, activities, worksheets, and college-planning resources.

*American higher education offers more colleges than any other system in the world, with more variety in disciplines and professional training, but a student who doesn't like the school she chose for her first year can, assuming she keeps her grades up, easily transfer. High school students who bite their tongues and actually listen to what college counselors say on this matter will learn that being crowned by Ivy has little, if any, bearing on whether they will fulfill their dreams of love, power and wealth. Character traits—such as persistence, optimism and honesty—established long before anyone takes the SAT or the ACT—are far more crucial.*

*— [Newsweek: How to Get into College, 2001 Edition]*

# Overview

The three primary areas of focus for a college-bound student are:

1. Meeting your high school graduation requirements.

2. Becoming a strong candidate for admissions to your first-choice colleges and being prepared to succeed academically once you get there.

3. Meeting your EFC (Expected Family Contribution) for college tuition, room, and board.

There will be two additional areas of focus for the recruited college-bound athlete:

4. Registering with the NCAA Clearinghouse and meeting the NCAA qualifications for a student-athlete.

5. Developing an athletic profile/portfolio specific to your sport.

# 1: develop a four-fold strategy

There are four broad categories that will ultimately determine how successful you are in developing your college-bound plan.

## Academics

- Meeting high school graduation requirements
- Meeting college admission standards
- Course work
- Grades
- Class rank
- High School Profile
- SAT I, SAT II, ACT, and AP exam scores
- Awards, honors, noteworthy academic achievements and recognition

# Extracurricular Activities

- Sports
- Clubs
- Student organizations
- Community service
- Volunteer hours
- Work experience

# Personal Qualities

- Essay
- Interview
- Recommendations
- Contribution to your school community
- Unique talent (e.g., artistic, music, athletic, dance, mathematic, or public speaking)
- Personal achievements (e.g., overcoming adversity, resiliency, integrity, worthy ideals, or innovation)

# Intangible and Other Influencing Factors

- Ethnicity

- Gender

- Socioeconomic background

- Geographical area

- Involvement in a club or activity for which the college has a unique need, e.g., genius-level I.Q., classical pianist, point guard, martial arts instructor, swimmer, or 400-meter sprinter

---

# 2: identify your dreams

---

What are your dreams and aspirations—the places you want to go, things you want to experience, changes you want to make in your home, community, or in the world itself? Where do you find your joy? What type of people do you prefer being around? What type of job would you do even if you did not get paid to do it? Or, better yet, what is your purpose? Are you passionate about music, art, science, math, sports, or social issues? Do you prefer working with people or in isolation? Do you have a passion to coach on the field or run front-office operations? Do you have a passion to teach elementary school children or inspire college students? Would you prefer to write a book, give a lecture, or both? Answering such questions as you enter high school will help you to identify the classes that will expand your knowledge, nurture your passions, and best prepare you for the college experience you are interested in pursuing.

## 3: identify your dream schools

1. Make a list of things you most enjoy doing, e.g., traveling, shopping, sports, surfing, roller skating, music, dressing up, dressing down, cooking, eating, telling jokes, talking on the phone, socializing, dancing, solving puzzles, writing poetry, drawing cartoons, playing computer games, lifting weights, studying

martial arts, running marathons, sailing, flying an airplane, camping, fishing, golfing, competing, creating, etc.

2.  Make a list of the type of people and places you enjoy, e.g., large crowds, small groups, debating/discussing political and social issues, attending concerts or sporting events, bodybuilding, theatrical performances, building businesses, working on an assembly-line, pursuing a spiritual journey, attending social functions, exploring and discovering, creating and developing, living in a penthouse, or living on a farm.

3.  Make a list of the types of careers that will allow you to do those things on your first list and work with the type of people or live in the places on your second list.

Rather than choosing Harvard, Yale, or Princeton because they are part of the Ivy League—MIT, Stanford, Cal Tech, or Duke because they are on everyone's top-ten list—Spelman, Fisk, Howard, or FAMU because they are some of the most renowned HBCUs—choose a college that will allow you to pursue your passions, surround you with the type of people you enjoy, and nurture your intellectual development, creative capacity, and social consciousness. In essence, carefully choose a place to live, grow, and enjoy life for the four years following high school.

# 4: know what makes you special

The question for you to ask yourself as you begin the process of developing your high school plan is, "Four years from now, why would a college want to admit me into its freshman class? What will be special about me and what will I be able to contribute to its school community?"

Asking that question as you enter high school will help you to better understand how to take advantage of the many programs and opportunities available at your high school and accessible to aspiring college students over the course of your four-year high school experience. Whether you are passionate about athletics, politics, dance, music, science, mathematics, journalism, poetry, art, philosophy, social issues, technology, or speech and debate, your high school years will have a significant impact on the scope and depth of the college application packages that you prepare as a high school junior and senior. Entering high school with the passionate desire to pursue something, become something, discover something, change something, or fulfill some purpose will guide your intellectual, spiritual, moral, physical, and creative development in ways, that, four years from now, will enable you to sit in a college interview and say, "I have had a passion to do ... since I entered high school; this is what I have done and why I want to continue my studies at your college."

The uniqueness of your school performance, extracurricular activities, standardized test scores, hobbies, interests, leadership abilities, personal achievements, race, gender, culture, family background, and life experiences not only define who you are, but make a statement as to why you are different.

# 5: build relationships

Developing and executing an effective high school plan will require that you build relationships with several groups of people. Colleges will evaluate your application in part based on recommendations from your teachers and counselor; your meaningful involvement in clubs, organizations, school and community service projects; and your involvement in sports, band, cheerleading, or other special-interest activities. The relationships you develop with tutors and study groups will also greatly contribute to your academic success throughout high school. Some of the people whom would make excellent sources of recommendations are:

- Teachers
- Faculty Advisors
- Clergy
- Law Enforcement

- Coaches
- Administrators
- Local Politicians
- An Alumnus

# 6: get organized

Preparing for the work ahead requires that you establish a place to store all of your high school information as well as all of the college and financial-aid information you gather over the next four years.

- Set up a 3-inch binder and label it "College Plan."

- Set up four file folders or boxes and label them:

  - Academics

  - Programs & Camps

  - Scholarships

  - Awards, Competitions, & Internships

- Set up two boxes and label them:

  - College Information

  - Financial-Aid Information

# 7: identify your team

If you are planning on going to college, then you need to affirm that you are going to college. This means that you have to begin talking about college to your family, friends, teachers, counselors, coaches, mentors, and tutors. The more you talk about college, the more information people with share with you. The more they will confirm or challenge what you think about college, what you are thinking about doing with your life, and whether or not what you are doing now is consistent with where you say you are planning to go.

Your high school counselor (or in some cases a mentor or private counselor) is going to be one of the most important people with whom to share your college dreams. Along with this book, he or she should become an invaluable source of information. It is your counselor's job to provide you with, or direct you to, the information you need to fulfill your college aspirations. Your counselor may be able to make your work a lot easier by identifying where to get the information you need, assisting in completing the necessary financial-aid forms, and ensuring you fulfill your high school graduation requirements. Eventually, you will have to turn your college application packages in to your counselor, who will have to order and enclose your high school transcript prior to mailing your materials to the colleges to which you apply.

Working with friends, booster clubs, mentoring programs, organizations, churches, and other families will allow you to accomplish much more than by working alone. Develop teams or committees to focus on specific areas:

- College Admissions
- College Fairs
- Scholarships
- Summer Camps
- Internships
- Recruited-athletes
- College Programs for Juniors and Seniors

- Special Interest Programs (e.g., athletics, arts, music, math, science, literary, leadership, etc.)
- Local, National, and International Competitions
- Tutors
- SAT I, SAT II, PSAT, and ACT Prep Programs
- Putting together the Application Packages

# 8: follow your stats

As you begin high school, imagine beginning an NBA or WNBA career. Every pass, steal, free throw, three-pointer, blocked shot, and playoff game—every statistic is going to become part of your permanent NBA/WNBA stat sheet. Your college application package will represent your high school stat sheet—SAT/ACT scores, class rank, GPA, course work, extracurricular activities, recommendation letters, job history, summer camps, special programs, the offices that you hold in clubs and organizations, and awards.

# Chapter 1

## *Academics*

There is a reason that the first area of focus in your high school plan is academics and not because it falls first in alphabetical order. Your high school transcript is the most important part of your application package. Whether you are a star athlete, president of the student council, brilliant musician, or most popular student in your high school, college success ultimately comes down to your ability to successfully complete the course work.

Athletics, leadership positions, creative or artistic talent, awards and community involvement may all influence the final decision of a college admissions committee; however, once you are accepted, you will have to complete the course work to receive your college degree. In the final analysis, your academic ability is still the most important aspect of your college preparation.

Your academic performance will include:

- Meeting high school graduation requirements (which may include passing high school exit exams)
- Meeting college admissions standards
- Course work, grades, class ranking, and high school profile
- SAT I, SAT II, ACT, AP, or IB exam scores
- Awards, honors, noteworthy academic achievements and recognition

# 9: maintain a college focus

It is important to begin high school with a college focus. Whether you are considering going into the military, pursuing a trade, or simply getting a job after high school, you should begin high school with a college focus. Doing so will ensure that you do as much as possible to prepare yourself for college should you decide to attend college after graduating from high school. While the primary focus of this book is on college admissions, keep in mind that for high school students, there are many postsecondary educational opportunities that may lead to something other than a four-year university. A student's passion for cooking may lead to a culinary school, a passion for computer programming may lead to a computer programming or technical school, a passion for a trade may lead to an internship or trade school.

# 10: research schools

As soon as you begin to develop an idea of the types of colleges in which you are interested, or colleges that offer fields of study in your areas of interest, begin making contact. Colleges keep track of whom, and how often, prospective students contact them. It is never too early in the process to let potential schools know that you have an interest in their programs. Write, call, or e-mail admissions, professors, coaches, departments, or programs to request information. Once you are in their database, they will begin mailing or e-mailing you information on a regular basis. As you begin receiving information, give extra or unwanted information to your high school counselor so that he or she may use it in the guidance office or counseling center.

# 11: develop a top-ten list

Your top-ten list of schools should reflect places and programs where you can envision yourself developing lasting relationships with professors as well as a desire to return to the campus to inspire hope in future students and share the sense of pride you should have in becoming one of your school's distinguished alumnus. Place your top-ten list in your school binder, on a wall, or onto your refrigerator— someplace where you will be continually reminded of your high school focus until you can begin checking off those schools where you have been accepted.

# Chapter 2

## *High School Graduation Requirements*

High school graduation requirements vary by state. Sometimes the requirements vary by district within the state and even by school within the district. It is important for you to identify and understand your state or school district's graduation requirements and track your progress throughout high school.

Fully understanding your high school course requirements will require that you meet with your counselor, read your school district's curriculum guide, and understand your state department of education's high school graduation course requirements, which will specify the number of classes that you must pass within such areas as math, English, science, social studies, foreign language, physical education, and electives.

# 12: identify exit exams

There are many well-publicized stories of students in states that require high school exit exams having their college-bound dreams deferred or destroyed as a result of their failure to pass the exams. At one Georgia high school, upwards of 70 percent of the students had A's and B's on their transcript and yet 90 percent of the students failed the End-of-Grade test in Algebra. In the state of Florida, many students are accepted into college, only to find that they must withdraw their application as a result of not being able to pass their high school exit exam. Do not take your high school graduation requirements for granted or assume that your classes or teachers have adequately prepared you. Meet with your counselor and get all the necessary information to ensure that you are fulfilling the graduation requirements in your school district and that you are enrolled in the necessary classes to prepare you for the end-of-grade exam or high school graduation tests in your state.

**BOSTON, Massachusetts (AP) -- Four attempts. Two points shy.**

The numbers plague Karl Kearns, a senior at Burke High School in Boston. This was the first year in which seniors statewide were denied diplomas if they failed the state's high school test, the Massachusetts Comprehensive Assessment System exam, or MCAS.

Kearns was one of some 4,800 seniors who didn't make the cut.

Despite maintaining a "B" average, winning an award for "most improved" in his class, being captain of his football team and overcoming the challenges of a broken home and a reading disability, he didn't score high enough to get a diploma and graduate with his classmates.

[AP Sunday, June 15, 2003]

### Diplomas Denied as Seniors Fail Exit Exams

This spring, thousands of high school seniors across the country weren't awarded a high school diploma because they failed to pass their state's exit exam. Lawmakers in states such as California, Florida, Massachusetts, Nevada, and North Carolina have instituted the high-stakes tests to ensure graduates are competent in basic skills, but now they face pressure from angry students and parents to delay or scrap the tests. Students say the tests do not reflect the curriculum covered in school.

"The stuff on the test doesn't equate to anything that I've learned in school," 18-year-old Robyn Collins of Sparks, Nevada protested to the Washington Post. A student with a solid academic record and a 3.0 grade point average, Collins had just failed on her fifth attempt to pass the math portion of the state's exit exam.

[School Reform News, September 1, 2003 ]

# 13: if you are an athlete

If you are planning on participating in college athletics during your freshman year in college, you must register with the NCAA Clearinghouse (www.ncaaclearinghouse.net). Many athletes register during the summer between their junior and senior year after receiving their junior-year high school transcript. The Clearinghouse outlines the full range of classes, grades, test scores, and recruiting guidelines.

Carefully review the *NCAA Guide for the College-Bound Student-Athlete* (ncaa.org) so you fully understand recruiting guidelines, eligibility requirements, and registration dates. It is possible to fulfill the graduation requirements for your high school and not meet the NCAA eligibility requirements, which would mean that you would not be able to receive a scholarship or be eligible to compete as a college student-athlete.

# Chapter 3

## *Course Work*

You and your parents must take an active role in planning, scheduling, and sequencing your high school classes. Class requirements vary by high school and can range from unrestricted open enrollment to highly restricted—highly selective student enrollment that requires counselor and teacher approval.

During eighth grade, your middle school counselor will submit a suggested class schedule to the high school that you will be attending. Nearing the end of eighth grade or during the summer before enrolling in high school, you will receive your high school class schedule. Carefully review your ninth-grade class schedule to ensure that you will begin on track toward taking the classes that you would like to take during your four years of high school.

# 14: take a challenging schedule

When planning your course schedule, do not be afraid to enroll in academically rigorous classes such as honors or AP classes. The sooner that you enroll in the higher-level classes, the more higher-level classes you will have the opportunity to take throughout high school. If you developed a challenging middle school course schedule, you may find yourself, as a high school freshman and sophomore, in higher-level math and science classes with juniors and seniors. Consider yourself fortunate to be as many as two years ahead and well on the way to developing an impressive high school transcript.

Students who choose to load their schedules with easy classes and electives severely limit their college choices. Admissions committees at the nation's top colleges will be looking for a challenging academic schedule and examples—either in your course work or in your teacher recommendations—of your participation in classroom discussions, debates, and active involvement in furthering ideas and opinions. Colleges want students who can contribute to classroom discussions, share ideas and opinions, and effectively communicate with instructors and classmates. Admissions officers at the top colleges are assigned to regions of the country. They are familiar with the high schools within their region and communicate with high school counselors. The admissions officer assigned to your region may ask your counselor whether or not you are taking the most demanding, very demanding, demanding, average, or a below-average class schedule. Keep in mind that a *demanding* class schedule for a student who is not involved in any extracurricular activities may be considered by an admissions officer as a *very demanding* schedule for a student who plays one or more varsity sports or is involved in clubs and student organizations.

# 15: know your high school

Admissions committees pay attention to the classes offered at your high school and those that you chose to take. Many of the colleges that you apply to will request from your school's counselor, a "School Profile," which outlines the types of classes offered, total number of available honors and AP classes, state ranking, average SAT I scores, etc. The college admissions committee will raise the question, "Did this student take the most challenging classes offered at his or her high school?"

# 16: honors classes

Admissions committees will assess a higher value to honors classes. Depending on the subject or teacher, the class may move at a faster pace, involve more work, or require more effort on the part of the student. As a result of the increased difficulty, many school districts provide additional points that are credited to the student's overall GPA. For example, a school district may award an additional 7 points to the class numerical grade for honors classes. In such classes, a final numerical grade of 70 would result in 77 being posted to the student's grade point average; 90 results in a 97; and 100 results in a 107. This procedure permits students on a 4.0 scale to post GPAs higher than the scale, e.g., 4.5, 4.7, etc.

# 17: AP classes

Advanced Placement, or what is more commonly referred to as 'AP' classes, is a program of college-level courses, offered as regular high school classes. Students who take such classes have the opportunity to receive advanced placement or college credit. The AP program is administered by the College Board (www.collegeboard.org).

AP classes are considered the most difficult and demanding high school classes and are designed to prepare students for AP exit exams. AP exams are administered once a year in May and usually take two to three hours to complete. While many students take the exams at the end of their senior year, it is advisable to take the exam as soon as possible after completing the AP course work.

# 18: joint enrollment

Joint Enrollment programs provide opportunities to enroll in college while completing high school. Joint enrollment programs will vary by state and by school district within the state.

Some of the benefits of joint enrollment classes are:

- they qualify for college credit with some also qualifying for high school credit, thereby allowing students to take college classes in place of certain high school classes.

- they are usually paid for by the state, college, or local school district.

- they provide students with an opportunity to experience college-level classes while still in high school, thereby helping them to know what to expect when they enroll in college full-time.

- they enhance a student's college application by indicating that the student is capable of college-level work and may provide early admissions preference at the joint enrollment college.

- they provide an opportunity for students to learn from college professors.

# 19: grades count!

If you have the academic ability to be an 'A' student, then be an 'A' student. If you are an athlete and your teammates do not take academic achievement seriously, do not allow them to keep you from performing at the level of your academic potential. Put yourself in the best possible position to qualify first, for admission, and secondly, for financial aid. Do not be among the thousands of students who do not pay attention to their GPA until their junior year. By then you have two years of grades that can either prop your GPA up or weigh it down.

# 20: class rank

Class rank is one of those very important, little discussed, statistics that you need to be aware. Some colleges establish their primary admissions criteria based on class rank (e.g., top 5 percent, top 10 percent, etc.). States such as California and Florida, guarantee resident-students, admission into the state's public universities based on the student's class ranking. One of the most highly-publicized states, Texas, has a law that guarantee's resident-students, who rank in the top ten percent of their high school's graduating class, admission into the student's choice of the state's public universities.

# Chapter 4

## *Academic Support*

As you enter high school, you must openly and honestly assess your strengths and weaknesses. Do you have difficulty with math? Is science one of your weakest areas? Do you struggle with doing research and writing papers? Are you having difficulty grasping a foreign language? Do not allow yourself to get off to a slow start and do not shrug off your weaknesses, "I am just not good at math." You must identify what and whom you need to ensure your academic success throughout high school. Do not make the mistake of believing that a music major will not have to succeed in college math or that an athlete will not have to write a college paper. Even a star athlete, concert pianist, or brilliant artist will need a solid academic foundation to succeed in and graduate from college.

# 21: join a study group

Since you are likely to join a study group in college, it would be a good idea to form study groups during high school. You may find them particularly beneficial in your more challenging classes—those classes or subjects where you are experiencing difficulty or have an acknowledged weakness.

# 22: get a tutor

Do not get left behind. You are not always going to make a connection with all of your teachers. Sometimes you will experience a teaching-style–learning-style match and at other times you will experience a teaching-style–learning-style mismatch. In classes like math and science, which are challenging subjects in themselves, you may find yourself experiencing difficulty fully understanding concepts or equations that are being covered. This does not necessarily have anything to do with your intelligence or the teacher's effectiveness. However, it is your grades that admissions officers are going to be reviewing so it is your responsibility to let the teacher know when you are having difficulty. If you continue to find yourself struggling, it is your responsibility to find a tutor. Oftentimes, a tutor will have more time to explain problems and concepts in greater detail than what the teacher covers in class.

# 23: join an academic club

Consider joining clubs related to your academic areas—science, math, computer programming, foreign language, etc. Students involved in these clubs have probably taken classes that you are going to take and will have comments and information about teachers, tutors, course content, and how to succeed.

# Chapter 5

## *Academic Honors*

Begin high school with a focus on the types of honors, awards, and recognition that you would like to receive. Each state, local district, and high school recognizes student achievement differently. Identifying the available awards as you enter high school will help you to establish goals that include awards in a broad range of areas. Many colleges are interested in developing a diverse and well-rounded college community. Keep in mind that no award or recognition is too small to be overlooked.

There are many opportunities for high school students to be recognized by their school, local community, local government, religious, civic, and professional organizations. To ensure that you do not miss anything when it is time to complete your college application, establish a routine of making note of your awards in your *College-Planning* binder and filing your award in your awards box immediately upon receiving or being notified of the award.

---

*Research Programs That Relate to Your Passions.*

*There are many local, state, national, and international academic and scholarship competitions that reflect a broad range of academic scholarship and student interests.*

*As there are local, state, national, and international competitions in dance and sports, there are programs and competitions that relate to a student's passion in math, science, literature, geography, speech and debate, and other academic areas.*

*[A High School Plan for Students with College-Bound Dreams, p. 103]*

---

# Chapter 6

## *Plan Your Schedule*

After familiarizing yourself with your school district's graduation requirements, types of diplomas offered, and the amount of academic preparation that your top-ten colleges want to see in students admitted into their freshman class, you must develop your four-year high school schedule accordingly. If you began your college planning in middle school, your high school schedule will represent the final four years of the seven-year schedule that you outlined in middle school. If you are only beginning the process of developing your high school schedule, then you should plan to discuss or revise your schedule as needed with your counselor or career advisor.

# 24: develop your 4-year schedule

You may find developing a high school schedule a more difficult task than developing a college schedule. In college, a student is likely to take no more than four or five courses per quarter or semester (at Dartmouth College, students take only three classes per quarter), whereas on a traditional high school schedule, a student is likely to take six to eight classes. Also, at many colleges, a student has the opportunity to sit in on classes for a week or more to determine if he or she likes the instructor or is really interested in the course, whereas high school students rarely have choices of teachers or the flexibility of sitting in on a class before making a commitment to taking the class.

Your high school class schedule should:

1. Meet the mandatory graduation requirements within your school district.

2. Reflect as many advanced classes, which you can handle, to maximize your GPA and achieve a higher class ranking.

3. Meet the mandatory admission requirements at the college(s) you are applying to (and the NCAA Clearinghouse requirements, if you are planning on becoming a student-athlete).

4. Demonstrate to a college admissions committee your willingness to challenge yourself by taking the most demanding classes offered in your high school.

5. Reflect electives that provide an underlying academic or special-interest focus area (e.g., art, music, dance, medicine, or sports law) that will support your college application or essay.

# 25: know your options

Most people think of summer school as being for students who are struggling. However, consider summer school as an opportunity to take classes that are required for graduation—World History, P.E., Health, electives, etc.—to free your schedule during the school year for additional math, science, language arts, honors, or AP classes. Classes in summer school may also be used as a means of meeting your graduation requirements by the end of your junior year or the first semester of your senior year. This approach allows for early graduation, early college enrollment, or internship opportunities. Discuss the full range of options with your counselor.

# 26: expand your options

Night school, junior college, or online programs may provide other opportunities to take required, elective, or special-focus classes. Some school districts offer online classes or have agreements with neighboring school districts offering such classes. Many students find the online learning experience an enjoyable and engaging one. Those students who spend a great deal of time on their computers playing video games or in chat rooms, may find themselves more engaged in online classes than in their regular classes. As in the case of summer school, night school, or junior college, online programs provide an opportunity to take a greater number of math, science, honors, or AP classes during the normal school year.

Other options to be considered include:

- Internships

- Independent study

- Taking the school's yearbook class, developing the school's web site, or working on the staff of the school newspaper

- Exchange programs with other schools

- Community-service projects

- Working on a political campaign

- Enrolling in an academic or pre-college camp

- Attending Space Camp

- After-school jobs that can be designed to become internships like working at a nail salon for entrepreneurial studies, working at a senior citizen home for nursing studies, designing brochures for graphic arts studies, or writing/publishing a book.

# 27: 9th grade

Beginning in 9th grade, take the most challenging classes. Whether you are one of those students who experience difficulty making the 9th-grade transition into high school or one of those students who immediately become involved in sports, student organizations, and extracurricular activities, you must develop the class schedule that is most appropriate for you. Consider all options when planning your course schedule so that you do not overburden yourself. Take the most challenging schedule, which you believe you can achieve the highest grades.

Most school districts require only two years of a foreign language, however, you should consider taking a foreign language during each of your four years of high school, culminating in an AP foreign language class. Take classes that improve your reading and writing skills. Classes in history, philosophy, and literature will strengthen your reading, writing, and language foundation. Enhance your thoughts, ideas, and communication skills by actively participating in class and group discussions. When you submit your college applications, you will be required to provide teacher recommendations. You want teachers to be able to recall your active participation in classroom discussions and allude to your insightful ideas and opinions.

During Spring Break, plan to get two SAT II subject-area books and study for two SAT II tests to be given in May. Pick your two best subjects. Identify a special-interest summer camp, college-bound camp, or summer-school program to strengthen or enhance one of more academic areas. Continue reading, writing, and further developing your communication skills. You will also benefit by beginning to study a SAT I vocabulary building book. Read newspapers, magazines, novels, and any other material that expands your vocabulary and comprehension skills.

# 28: 10th grade

Carefully select among honors and AP classes available to sophomores at your school. However, do not take such a rigorous course schedule that you cannot play a sport or become involved in other student or extracurricular activities. Colleges will look for students who were academically challenged as well as students who contributed to their school community through sports, student government, extracurricular activities, and community service participation. Try to put yourself on track toward AP U.S. History in the 11th grade and AP Literature or College English by the 12th grade. You also want to continue in higher-level math and science classes.

Plan to take the SAT I, ACT, and PSAT. All your scores will help to identify your strengths and weaknesses. Remember that your 11th-grade PSAT scores will be used to qualify for National Merit or National Achievement

Scholar recognition.

By Spring Break, begin preparing for at least two more SAT IIs. Again, choose your best subjects. Use the summer months to continue strengthening your areas of interests and preparing yourself academically for the challenging classes that you plan to take during your junior year. Continue summer camp or summer-school opportunities to push yourself academically.

# 29: 11th grade

Hopefully you will be on track to take a full schedule of the most demanding classes available at your high school during your junior and senior years. Your advanced course schedule should have prepared you to do well on the SAT I, ACT, and PSAT. Begin working on your application and financial-aid essays. If you have enrolled in an English, language arts, or writing class, your teacher may be willing to critique your essays. Identify any remaining SAT IIs that are required by the colleges on your top-ten list. If you have met their requirements, then plan to take two more SAT IIs in your favorite subjects. Many colleges may require one specific SAT II and allow you to submit two or three of your choice. You want to submit your highest scores. Plan to take any final SAT IIs in May or June.

# 30: 12th grade

Avoid believing that taking a challenging course load in 9th through 11th grade allows you to take easy classes during your senior year. A bodybuilder would not maintain a healthy diet, five-day-a-week workouts, and extensive cardiovascular training, only to take a year off. One year off may take three years to regain his or her physique, form, and muscular definition. Your rigorous high school schedule has been designed not simply to get you admitted into college, but to succeed once you get there.

# 31: meet with your counselor

Meet with your counselor to ensure that you fully understand the opportunities at your high school. Following, are some questions to assist in guiding your discussions with your high school career or guidance counselor:

1. What are the required and recommended courses —for graduation and for college prep?

2. Are there any automatic admissions criteria for state colleges, for example, class rank?

3. Which elective courses do you recommend?

4. I have indicated the honors or AP courses that I am interested in taking and I would like to know if there is anything that I must do to meet all the prerequisites or enrollment requirements?

5. Can any of my elective or required classes be taken in summer school, night school, or online?

6. Are there tutors or is there a school-sponsored tutorial program that you would recommend?

7. What are your thoughts on the four-year schedule that I have developed?

8. When is the PSAT/NMSQT given?

9. Are there any after-school, evening, or special classes available for college planning or SAT I/ACT preparation?

10. Do you have college handbooks or other guides that I may browse or borrow? Do you have a copy of the free "Taking the SAT I" booklet that has a practice test in it?

11. Do you have a college-planning guide or calendar that outlines the types of things that I should be doing each year?

12. Is there a list of colleges that have a relationship with this school or actively recruit from this school?

13. Are there any college fairs at this school or nearby? And, if so, how can I find out when they are scheduled?

14. What are the requirements or standards for the honor society?

15. What clubs, organizations, community service, or student activities do you suggest that I consider joining or becoming involved in?

16. I have developed my top-ten list of schools. Do you have any information or are there any alumni from our school who can provide me with information about any of the schools on my list?

17. Are there any special scholarships or awards that I should be aware of that I can begin preparing myself?

18. How does our school compare to others, in terms of test scores, reputation, and ranking?

19. What is the deadline for submitting class requests for the next school year?

# Chapter 7

## *Standardized Testing/Exit Exams*

- **PSAT:** 9th, 10th, 11th grades (October)

- **SAT I (also called the SAT Reasoning Test):** Offered several times a year

- **SAT II:** Subject tests that you should take close to completing the respective subject

- **ACT:** Offered five times a year

- **AP Exam:** Given in May

- **EOCT:** End-of-Course-Tests, if required by state

- Graduation Tests, if required by state

# 32: SAT/ACT prep

Perhaps the biggest problems that students encounter, are, that they do not effectively prepare and they take required tests too late. As soon as you are prepared to take the SAT I or ACT, take them.

College admissions committees are trying to eliminate as many applications as possible to get to the right class size. Many colleges will eliminate thousands of applications to arrive at a class size of a few hundred students. Standardized test scores provide admissions committees with an easy way to eliminate applications.

- If your school offers a test preparation class, take it.

- If your school does not offer a class, find a free class at a local library, church, YMCA, or Boys and Girls Club.

- If you cannot find a free class, find one that you can afford being offered by one of the private companies.

- If you cannot find a free class and you cannot afford to pay for one, pick up a test preparation book at the bookstore or local library and go onto the Internet and do a search for "SAT I/ACT practice tests" and prepare yourself.

Take the SAT I as early as your sophomore year—certainly by your junior year—to get your first assessment as to whether or not your scores qualify for admission into your top-ten schools. If you are not satisfied with your scores, consider taking the test again, concentrating on one section (i.e., critical reading and writing, or the math). Hopefully, by concentrating your test preparation efforts on one section of the test, you will be prepared to take the test a third and final time, concentrating on the other section. Most colleges will accept the highest scores for each section, even if the tests were taken on different dates. Applying yourself and putting forth the effort to do your best work in your middle school and high school language arts and math classes will greatly enhance your preparation for the SAT I and ACT.

For students who are on an advanced math track, reviewing Algebra I, Algebra II and Geometry before taking the SAT I and ACT is excellent preparation. Reviewing an SAT I vocabulary book is also a good idea.

# 33: know the tests

## ACT (a perfect score is 36)

The ACT (American College Testing Exam) is a national college admission examination that consists of tests in English, Mathematics, Reading, Science, and an optional Writing section.

ACT results are accepted by virtually all U.S. colleges and universities. The ACT includes 215 multiple-choice questions and takes approximately three hours and 30 minutes to complete with breaks.

**Your score is based on the number of correct answers only, so if you are not sure, taking a guess does not hurt.**

## PSAT (a perfect score is 80)

The PSAT (Preliminary Scholastic Achievement Test) consists of two 25-minute verbal sections, two 25-minute math sections, and one 30-minute writing skills section. The PSAT provides practice for the SAT I, an evaluation of your abilities in comparison with other college-bound students, an opportunity to enter scholarship competitions, a chance to learn about colleges interested in students with a profile similar to yours, and qualifies students for National Merit and National Achievement Scholarship consideration.

As a result of your answers to the PSAT questionnaire, you will begin receiving college information in the mail so be sure to answer the questions carefully and provide an accurate mailing address. The PSAT score range is between 20 and 80.

**Junior-year scores are used to determine qualification for the National Merit and National Achievement Scholar programs.**

## SAT I (a perfect score is 2400)

The first SAT I (Scholastic Aptitude Test) was administered in 1926 to 8,040 students. Today more than two million students annually take the SAT I. The most recent change to the SAT I occurred in 2005. The Verbal Section was replaced with the Writing and Critical Reading Sections. The Writing Section consists of a 35-minute multiple-choice section and a 25-minute essay. The Critical Reading Section consists of two 25-minute and one 20-minute sections. The Math Section consists of two 25-minute and one 20-minute sections. The SAT I is offered during October, November, December, January, March, May, and June.

**The SAT carries a wrong answer penalty (either 1/4 or 1/3 point) with no deduction for blank answers.**

While most colleges will allow students to combine their highest scores from different SATs—that is, their best Writing, Critical Reading, and Math scores—admissions officers receive all of your scores.

## SAT II (a perfect score is 800)

The SAT II consists of 22 tests offered in five subject areas that are one-hour, mostly multiple-choice tests, designed to measure how much students know about a particular academic subject and how well they can apply that knowledge. Colleges use the test scores primarily for class placement; however, up to three tests may be required for some college admissions. The SAT II is offered during October, November, December, January, May, and June.

## CLEP (College-Level Examination Program)

CLEP is the College-Level Examination Program that provides students with the opportunity to demonstrate college-level achievement through a program of exams in undergraduate college courses. There are 2,900 colleges that grant credit or advanced standing for CLEP exams. Each college publishes its qualifying criteria and number of credits awarded. The qualifying criteria and credits awarded will vary by college.

# Chapter 8

## *Extracurricular Activities*

Many of the country's top students, with top grades and top SAT/ACT scores, do not get admitted into their first-choice colleges. Unfortunately, many of the top students are working so hard academically that they cannot find time to become involved in their school or community. It seems unfair that colleges want both scholarly students and students who are well rounded as a result of their athletic, extracurricular activities, or community service involvement. However, that is exactly what they want.

There is no perfect GPA, SAT/ACT scores, and extracurricular activity balance. Therefore, live your life! Play the sports that you enjoy, become involved in those student organizations that reflect your passions and interests, and perform community service because it is the right thing to do! College admissions officers are likely to value your passion, compassion, and contributions to your school or community.

## 34: make a contribution

As you explore the wide range of extracurricular activities available, both at your high school and within community, civic, or clerical organizations, pay special attention to opportunities that can eventually lead to scholarship consideration. The obvious possibilities relate to athletics; however, there are many not-so-obvious opportunities that increase your chances of receiving a wide range of scholarship awards.

- Student Government
- Creative/Performing Arts
- Science/Research Projects
- Community Service
- Speech and Debate
- Faith-based Programs

# 35: do something noteworthy

Academic preparation and standardized test scores have been covered in great detail because they undoubtedly are at the top of your stat sheet. They are the first things that the admissions officer will see and oftentimes will determine whether or not your application is rejected outright before he or she has had an opportunity to get to know who you are and the contribution you can make to his or her college community. If you make the first cut, your application will then be in a pile among hundreds, if not thousands, of other applications from students who are also academically qualified. It is at this point that who you are, what your interests are, and what contribution you can make to the college during your four years there and in society afterwards, will influence whether or not you are admitted.

- Sports
- Community Service
- Clubs
- Volunteer Hours
- Student Organizations
- Work Experience

True leadership, is not reflected in how many offices you hold or the number of organizations you can claim membership, but by who you are and how your school, family, friends, and community have benefited from your skills, talents, gifts, abilities, and compassion. School districts spend huge amounts of money teaching character values to elementary and middle school students; now, as a high school student, you have the choice of standing for something or falling for anything. If your friends encourage rebellion against your parents or mean-spirited behavior toward other students, you have the opportunity to define yourself and discover your purpose—not as a sheep in the herd but as a shepherd of the herd, not as a goose on a mindless migration but as an eagle soaring high above the clouds.

Admissions officers are interested in not only that you played a sport, but that you were willing to accept the responsibility of being the captain or co-captain of the team, organized a study hall, tutored other players, or encouraged teammates to focus on their academic preparation with the same passion as they prepared for athletic competition. An admissions officer is interested in not only that you belonged to organizations but that your involvement resulted in meaningful contributions through innovation, creativity, and collaboration. When you submit your college essays and you are asked for words that describe your character, you will want such words as integrity, perseverance, compassion, collaboration, self-motivation, responsibility, and respect to reflect who you are and what you stand for.

## 36: be involved in activities

Identify the full range of extracurricular activities (i.e., sports, clubs, organizations, community service, etc.) available at your high school and pick at least two you are willing to commit to for four years. Colleges are interested in your *commitment* and *contribution* to your activities. The greater the number of years that you demonstrate involvement in a particular activity, the more supportive it will be of your overall college application.

If some of the schools on your top-ten list are exclusive or highly-competitive colleges, then do some research and identify the clubs, student activities, or student organizations that are important to each school. Join one of the clubs or student organizations that would be highly thought of at your first-choice school and prepare to mention your involvement on your essay and during your interview. Otherwise, join a club or participate in an activity that you will enjoy and make a contribution that can be mentioned prominently on your college application and in your personal bio.

# 37: perform community service

Identify a community service project that would be of value to your community and that you would enjoy. Consider your personal areas of interest and ask the question, "How can I do what I enjoy and use it to benefit my country, church, school, or community?" Also, consider becoming involved with a local sorority or fraternity, Big Brothers Big Sisters, civic, community, or mentoring organization.

# 38: consider a sport

Athletics is one of the important parts of the college experience. Interest by a college coach for an intercollegiate sport or by an admissions committee for your potential contribution to the school's intramural sports programs may have a significant impact on your admissions status. If you have athletic abilities, you should consider developing them as a means of helping you to gain college admission or possibly receiving a full or partial scholarship to offset the costs of college tuition, fees, room, and board.

Set yourself apart from other athletes. Consider less popular sports like water polo, Nordic skiing, rowing, and fencing. Colleges oftentimes recruit scholarship athletes from outside of the United States, due to low interest in these types of sports by American high school students.

# 39: consider clubs and/or band

Choosing a club, organization, or student activity should reflect your interest and enhance your college plan. Just because a club or organization does not have much student interest at your high school does not mean that your involvement will not generate interest from colleges. For example, if the student government at your high school does not generate much student interest, your becoming involved and assuming a leadership position is impressive on your college application, even if it is not highly thought of in your high school. Any time there is a weak club or organization that does not generate a lot of student interest, you should see it as an opportunity. If you can revitalize a student activity or organization at your high school, church, or community organization, you will have a powerful story to tell on your college or scholarship essay and to share during a college interview.

Identify all the clubs and student organizations available at your high school, even those that you may not be interested in, at this time. As you move forward with developing your college plan, you may find that becoming involved in some of the clubs or organizations that you may not be interested in at this time may be important to helping you to be accepted into the college of your choice.

Playing a musical instrument and being a member of a successful marching band will oftentimes provide as much exposure as being a varsity athlete. Many colleges have stronger band traditions than they do athletic traditions and may actively recruit band members and award many band scholarships. At many colleges, fans attend football games with a stronger interest in the halftime show than in the game itself. While sports like basketball may have 12 players on a team, the college band may have over 200 members. Similar opportunities apply to cheerleading.

# 40: community involvement

Mentoring programs, community involvement programs, character development, student-student tutoring, designing sets for the drama department, taking photographs for the yearbook, recording statistics for the football team, running the concession stands, selling spirit wear, raising money for charities, building homes for Habitat for Humanity, all provide opportunities to enhance your college application and make a positive contribution to your high school and surrounding community. These kinds of involvement also provide opportunities to be formally recognized (another way of enhancing your college application).

Make a list of the programs and activities, which you are currently involved or have an interest in becoming involved. Keep in mind that there is always an opportunity for you to begin a new program at your high school or in your community.

# 41: competitions

Competitions provide additional opportunities to earn scholarship money, local and national recognition, and further enhance a college application. Competitions are available in athletic programs, cheerleading, band, academic areas, the arts, and a number of student-interest areas. Begin identifying the competitions that you may be interested in entering. Keep track of your participation and any awards that you receive.

# 42: get a job

Instead of bagging groceries, explore employment opportunities within areas of interest or areas that provide practical applications for some of your school course work. Following, are examples of employment opportunities that relate to classes:

- *Typing:* Secretarial, office assistant, general office

- *Art:* Flyers, store window themes, brochures, signs

- *Weight Training:* Assisting personal trainers, stacking weights at a health club

- *Speech & Debate:* Sales, telemarketing, customer service

- *Math:* Accounting, tax preparation assistance, bookkeeping

- *Science:* Veterinarian's office, dental office, drug-store sales

# Chapter 9

## *Personal Qualities*

No matter how you compare to others in terms of grades and test scores, who you are, what you have done, and what you stand for can become the defining factor that convinces an admissions officer that you are a student who would make a noteworthy contribution to his or her college community. Each day throughout your high school years you have the opportunity to separate yourself from the masses and define yourself. More than trying to make yourself into something, allow the divinely unique person whom you were created to be to come to the surface. Do not try to blend in and be like everyone else. Allow the divinely unique you to blossom. Not only will you distinguish yourself from the thousands of other applicants, but you will more likely identify the college community that would provide the best environment to nurture your artistic, personal, intellectual, and spiritual growth.

# 43: be a leader

Colleges are looking for leaders—students who can contribute to intellectual discussions, challenge professors, create music, explore science, provide creative and intellectual insight into the issues of today and contribute to their communities.

Assess if you have been developing your leadership skills:

- Have you contributed to the creation of a new student club or organization?

- Have you been elected into office or served in a leadership capacity in an organization?

- Have you made a meaningful contribution to your school or community?

- Have you created a new approach or implemented a new way of doing things that has enhanced your school, church, or community?

- Have you taught, tutored, coached, inspired, or encouraged others?

- Have you taken something that you have learned through a classroom experience and applied it through the creation of a new product or new way of doing things?

- Have you led a social cause or publicly lobbied for a legislative change?

# 44: define your character

Your character defines who you are, what you stand for, and the beliefs and principles that guide your life. Do not allow yourself to be influenced by mean-spirited, self-centered, obnoxious people who go out of their way to ridicule, take advantage of, and hinder others. Do not follow the crowd or allow such people to define your character. What are your values, beliefs, and guiding principles? Take a moment and write down five values that define who you are. Ultimately, a person will be known by his or her works. If these values truly define who you are in the ninth grade, then they will be evident in your works by the time you write your college essays in the eleventh and twelfth grades.

Many colleges will require teacher recommendations. Teachers will be asked to share their comments and insight into your personality and academic ability. Some schools will provide teachers with a checklist to rate such qualities as:

- personality
- curiosity
- academic promise
- self-confidence
- warmth of personality
- concern for others

# 45: get to know 3 teachers

Over the course of your four years of high school, take the time to get to know at least three teachers—people who would value the opportunity to write a letter telling the world what a wonderful person you are and attesting to your character and academic ability. Keep in mind that over the course of four years of high school, your participation in classroom discussions, contribution to group projects, and involvement in clubs and student organizations will provide many opportunities to develop relationships and contribute in a meaningful and relevant way to your school community. Admissions officers will view your involvement in your high school as indicative of your potential involvement in the vibrant life of their college community, which will offer an even broader range of clubs and organizations.

# 46: do not get suspended

To take full advantage of the range of high school opportunities, you have to take your school's policies and procedures seriously. Discipline infractions not only disrupt the high school experience for classmates, interfere with classroom instruction, and contribute negatively to your school's overall school climate and culture but may cause you to forfeit your opportunity to participate in extracurricular activities, student organizations, or keep you from being recommended for programs and awards that would otherwise enhance your college application package.

Your high school record may contain a complete listing of your discipline infractions for each year of high school. You do not want to allow a split-second decision in the ninth grade to hinder your college application in the twelfth grade.

# Chapter 10

## *Intangibles*

Intangibles represent all of those areas not previously covered, which contribute to your uniqueness:

- Where you live

- Ethnicity, gender, and family structure

- Legacy status

- Experiences and circumstances

Your geographical area and community setting will have an impact on your application. Colleges typically seek to develop a diverse freshman class of students from different geographical regions—throughout the United States and other countries, and types of communities—urban, suburban, rural, liberal, conservative, etc. While in-state tuition is usually substantially less at public universities than out-of-state tuition, you may be more easily accepted to an out-of-state college looking for students from your geographical region.

# 47: understand your competition

As colleges look for geographical diversity, they also look to develop well-balanced classes representing ethnic, gender, cultural, and socioeconomic diversity. If you are from an affluent background, you may have more competition being accepted into some of the top schools where large numbers of students from similar socioeconomic backgrounds apply, whereas a student from a working-class or poor family may be among only a few applicants from similar socioeconomic backgrounds.

Another example would be an African-American male student applying to Morehouse College, an all-male historically black college. He will find himself competing for admissions with thousands of students from very similar backgrounds.

A student from a migrant family who is forced to move frequently and enroll into a number of schools and school districts has a very different educational experience than a student from a middle-class family of professional parents in a stable home environment. If both students develop similar academic credentials and test scores, the migrant student clearly has done so while having to overcome a more difficult set of circumstances than the middle-class student.

The question that you must ask is, "If there is a large number of applications from students who have a similar ethnic, socioeconomic, and family background as myself, what can I do to distinguish myself?"

# 48: celebrate your experiences

Your experiences, such as where you have traveled, the type of communities where you have lived, the organizations that you have been involved with, and programs or camps in which you have participated contribute to your intangibles. Your family experiences have uniquely contributed to who you are, whether your parents are millionaires or migrant workers, serving in law enforcement or political office, delivering mail or delivering babies, researching environmental issues or performing landscaping, teaching students in regular classrooms or prison inmates, serving children in school cafeterias or serving parishioners in a congregation. These are the roots from which you have sprung and the experiences which provide the substance of your hopes, dreams, perspective, and perception of the world around you. Whether from privilege or from the projects, there is no shame in where you hail from; all geographical areas, ethnicity, and socioeconomic backgrounds reflect the diversity of the global landscape.

# 49: choose the right school

Your passionate areas of interest contribute to your uniqueness and may enhance the diversity of a college community. Do you teach martial arts? Do you coach little league baseball? Do you run a soccer clinic for inner-city kids during the summer? Do you volunteer for political campaigns? Are you a tutor in a literacy program at the Boys and Girls Club? Such programs, involvement, and areas of interest help to shape your uniqueness. Many students will apply to colleges because of the college's rank or status. Such students are more concerned with getting admitted into a prestigious college than they are with pursuing some particular area of interest, dream, or aspiration. Your passionate interests and continued pursuit of your dreams and aspirations will separate your application from that of the masses.

Align your areas of interest with a college major. Use your research to assess the college's commitment to your field of study and its student diversity needs. For example, a female student interested in pursuing such majors as engineering, mathematics, or science, which typically have fewer female applicants, may find herself more aggressively recruited than female students interested in pursuing nursing, which has a large number of female applicants.

Students who have demonstrated a passion for art or music stretching back to elementary school may have an advantage over students who say that they are interested in pursing art but took their first art class as a high school senior.

# 50: plan your summers

The summer months between 8th grade and your senior year of high school should not be squandered. Take advantage of the many opportunities to explore your talents, interests, and abilities. Some of the many opportunities that you may explore, experience, or become involved in are:

- Traveling

- Working in a meaningful job related to an area of interest or through an internship

- Participating in a summer learning opportunity in an academic, artistic, or community service

- Participating in pre-college summer camps/programs

- Participating in an AAU, USATF, or club sport

- Participating in summer practice for a high school sport such as football, cross country, lacrosse, soccer, swimming, etc.

- Volunteering as a counselor, life guard, coach, or art instructor at a parks and recreation, Boys and Girls Club, or community program

- Taking some of your non-academic classes or electives in summer school to open your schedule for more honors or AP classes during the regular school year

- Starting a business or working on a special project

Unlike the summer months during elementary and middle school, this is not the time to relax at grandma's house sitting back and watching television or playing video games. The summer months provide opportunities to attend camps or summer school, compete in AAU or USATF sports competitions, pursue internships, or otherwise engage in programs or opportunities that will enhance your college application package.

# 51: attend a camp or internship

There are many summer enrichment, internship, and college program opportunities. The first two stops are your high school counselor's office and the Internet. Research programs related to your areas of interest and utilize the opportunity to increase your academic, athletic, or creative skills. Try to concentrate first and foremost on those areas that relate directly to your college interests, whether in your major field of study or in sports that you intend to pursue on the college level.

# Chapter 11

## *Your Essay*

Do not take your essay likely; it may represent the most important part of your entire application package. It will provide your opportunity to define who you are and state your case for admission into the college to which you are applying. It can take away from or enhance the overall picture of who you are, what you stand for, and why the admissions committee should give you an opportunity ahead of the thousands of other applicants. This is your opportunity to explain your grades; share your convictions, beliefs, philosophies, and guiding principles; tell what you know about the college's values, beliefs, and traditions; and merge your hopes, dreams, and aspirations.

Imagine your essay standing on a stage. The curtain pulls back and your essay walks from center stage to the podium. The spotlight shines, but there is talking and lack of interest throughout the room as thousands of other essays whisper, motion, and scream for attention, yet it is your essay standing alone at the podium as a Sunday morning preacher.

*"I ain't where I wanna be,*

*I ain't where I oughta be,*
*I ain't where I need to be,*
*But thank God,*
*I ain't where I was."*

There is silence throughout the auditorium as all voices and distractions quiet. All discourse, debate, and discussions become still as a lake beneath the moonlight, as your essay captures, captivates, and continues a brilliant oratory on your behalf—sharing your hopes and your dreams, your achievements and your aspirations, your frailties and your uniqueness—your essay is the single ripple on the water carrying your message as the ripples widen and spread into the spirit, soul, and consciousness of the listener.

# 52: practice, practice, practice

An important part of the process of preparing and practicing requires that you read other essays. What you learn from reading good essays and bad essays can help you to create a great essay. Your goal from the beginning must be to create a great essay—not merely a good one but a best seller—one that will leave a lasting impression. The essay is such an important component of your college admissions and scholarship application that you should not wait until the last minute to begin writing. Good essays are written months, if not years, in advance.

1. Practice.

2. Read other essays.

3. Read as many essay-preparation books as you need in order to understand the essay-writing process.

4. Write essays for extra credit throughout middle and high school and allow your teachers to assist with editing, grammar, punctuation, style, and content.

5. Keep in mind the basic admissions officer's question, "What does this applicant offer our college?"

---

# 53: tell your story

---

The sooner that you begin to assess your life based on some of the important essay themes, the faster you will begin to explore the important things about yourself and your character, the obstacles that you have had to overcome and what makes you uniquely the person that you are. A good essay written along the following themes can make a lasting impression on the readers of your essay:

- Hard work

- Overcoming obstacles

- Being of service

- Teamwork
- Perseverance
- Individual initiative
- Passion and enthusiasm
- Responsibility
- Civic duty
- Purpose
- Character or core value
- Autobiography
- Person you most admire
- Major challenge in your life
- Something significant that you want to accomplish
- Your strengths and weaknesses
- An issue of personal, local, national, or international concern
- Actions you would take if you were in a position of leadership, e.g., politician, principal, CEO, etc.

# 54: identify your heroes/heroines

- What stories have you read of leadership, personal sacrifice, or service that have inspired you?

- What people have demonstrated, through their lives or their ability to overcome obstacles, an example that you wish to follow?

- What people have left a legacy that has provided an example of the values that humanity should aspire toward?

- What people embody the values, beliefs, and ideals that define who you are or what you aspire to become?

- What people have, through their thoughts, words, or deeds, changed the course of human history in a meaningful and relevant way?

- With which historical figures would you value the opportunity to sit and discuss ideas, opinions, and views on the most pressing social or political issues of the day?

Make a list of the people whom you most admire in such areas as:

- Family or community

- Historical figures

- Political, civic, business, or religious leaders

- Educators (i.e., teachers, counselors, administrators, or coaches)

- Athletes, entertainers, and public figures

- Everyday people, e.g., custodians, cafeteria workers, farmers, brick masons, waiters or waitresses

# 55: get help

The reason that you want to begin experimenting with your essay writing in your early years of middle and high school is that it is an important skill to develop. You will benefit, for not only your college applications and scholarship submissions, but, for the reading and writing components of the PSAT, SAT I, and ACT as well as preparation for the writing component of high school exit exams. This is your future. You must passionately share your story. It does not matter how well or badly written the first drafts of your essays are. You have your English, language arts, and literature teachers to edit, critique, and provide invaluable feedback. You may even be able to earn extra credit for some of your writing. The way to become good at writing is to write often and to develop a willingness to accept constructive criticism.

# 56: carefully choose your words

Passion • Purpose • Perseverance • Compassion • Integrity • Diligence • Respect • Responsibility • Determination • Persistence • Dedication • Devotion • Commitment • Enthusiasm • Energy • Fortitude • Kindness • Humanity • Generosity • Selflessness • Tolerance • Awareness • Service • Sense of duty • Leadership • Teamwork • Cooperation

• Humor • Originality • Innovation • Imagination •
Thoughtful • Judgment • Independence • Honor • Morality
• Resilience • Experimentation • Idealism • Vision •
Mission • Conceptualized • Created • Explored • Pursued •
Discovered • Developed • Taught • Trained • Coached • Led
• Reformed • Established • Initiated • Tutored • Founded
• Felt obligated • Collaborated with • Entrepreneurship •
Was responsible for

# 57: create a quality essay

Do not just sit down and start writing. Take the time
to prepare yourself mentally and identify the necessary
resources to develop a well-thought-out and well-written
essay. When your essay steps to the podium, you do not
want a hair out of place, food between his or her teeth, mud
on his or her shoes, her slip showing, or his fly opened! You
do not want anything to take away from the oratory. When
you submit your essay, make it the best and highest quality.

You will not be there to explain errors, mistakes, smudges, stains, or anything that will distract the listener from hearing your story and getting to know your hopes and your dreams. Before you submit your essay, find the person who never likes anything that you do—the one person who is always critical—and allow him or her to read your essay to see if he or she can find anything wrong. Invite the person to "let you have it," to be as critical as possible. If you can win him or her over, you are on your way to submitting an outstanding essay.

Although previously stated, the point bears repeating that you should write your essay days, weeks, or even months in advance so that you can read it, have someone else read it, have a teacher proof it, and then read it again. Even after all the reading, you will find that you used "if" when you meant "of" or "and" when you meant "an" or "he" when you meant "the." Each time you read your essay, you are likely to find a misplaced or misused word. The one thing that you never want to find is a misspelled word!

# Chapter 12

## *Financial Aid/Scholarships*

Acquiring the needed financial aid to pay for the cost of college can be as simple as meeting state qualifying standards (such as obtaining a 3.0 GPA in a Georgia high school and qualifying for Georgia's Hope Scholarship to be used at Georgia colleges), as time-consuming as combing through the many scholarship books and web sites, or simply paying private scholarship consultants. Putting together your financial-aid treasure chest will require that you determine the best strategy for you based on your family's needs and your top-ten list of colleges.

Gen and Kelly Tanabe in the book, *How to Find Great Scholarships,* note:

*When we were searching for scholarships, we found them in nearly every place imaginable. Some we discovered in the dusty collection of books at our library. Others by serendipitous newspaper announcements of past winners. We even found an award advertised on a supermarket shopping bag.*

*Having personally spent hundreds of hours scouring the planet for scholarships and meeting dozens of other successful scholarship winners, we have learned where most scholarships are hidden.*

## 58: set aside two boxes

- One box for the scholarships that you apply to which will contain your essays and necessary application information

- The second box for your overflow of scholarship information that you may not be considering at this time

# 59: start early

The important thing is to start early so that one at a time becomes hundreds of entries by the time college enrollment comes around.

# 60: get a permanent address

We live in a transient society. Jobs change, students transfer to different schools, apartment leases expire, families lose their homes or purchase new homes. Once you begin applying for scholarships, your name and address will find its way onto many different mailing lists and into many different scholarship databases. You are going to begin receiving lots of mail. You need a stable address for the next FOUR years! We have a P.O. Box. No matter where we move, we will keep the same P.O. Box so that we do not miss an opportunity. Do not run the risk of changing your address before the big scholarship award comes in.

## 61: get a high speed connection

There are more scholarships available on the web—more information and applications that can be downloaded than you will ever have the time to research. You have to invest in an Internet access account and a high-speed connection, i.e., DSL, Cable, Satellite, etc. Many students do all of their research on the Internet. Get as much computer power as you can afford—the fastest processor, largest hard disk, and fastest connection. You will also need a fast printer. There will be lots of files to download and forms to print.

## 62: organize your paperwork

Get your essays and paperwork together. Most scholarships only require that you complete an application, write an essay, include some paperwork, and submit the package by the deadline. Keep all of your original documents filed neatly in a box and keep copies in a binder under the appropriate tabs like grades, test scores, transcript, letters of recommendation, financial records, awards, essays, summaries of your extracurricular activities, etc.

# 63: be patient and encouraging

There are some mandatory forms that you must complete so now is a good time to become familiar with completing the forms. The experience will also help you to understand what information—tax forms, social security numbers, employment income, assets, liabilities, etc.,—is going to be required. If you or your parents treasure your privacy, then you are about to discover that your financial life is going to become an open book. The most important thing for you to keep in mind is do not guess. Also, do not lie! Get your facts straight and answer all of the questions truthfully.

1.  Get a copy of the *Common Application* at *www.commonapp.org/* and complete it fully. The information that you provide on the Common Application will be referred to as you complete the many scholarship applications over the next four years.

2.  Get a copy of the *FAFSA* (Free Application for Federal Student Aid) at *www.fafsa.ed.gov/* and complete it fully. This is the application that the federal government and your college will use to determine your eligibility for financial aid and the amount of aid that you are able to receive.

3.  Submit your *FAFSA* as soon as possible after January 1 of your senior year. Expect to receive a SAR (Student Aid Report) in about four to six weeks after submitting your FAFSA. THIS WILL BECOME YOUR MOST IMPORTANT FINANCIAL-AID DOCUMENT— DO NOT LOSE IT!

4. Get a copy of *Funding Your Education*, a free publication from the U.S. Department of Education at *www. studentaid.ed.gov*. From the web site you can also set up a student financial-aid web account to assist in developing your financial-aid plan based on your current year in school.

5. Contact your state finance commission (e.g., Georgia Student Finance Commission) and request all available financial-aid information.

# 64: identify yor niche

While you should apply for all types of general scholarships, identify the areas in which you uniquely qualify. Do you, for example, have special interests—art, web-page design, animation, film, drama, poetry, short stories, journalism, photography, etc.? Belong to a particular ethic group? Low income? Is anyone in your family a member of a particular religious group, professional organization, fraternity, sorority, or fraternal organization like the Masons or Shriners? Are you an athlete? Have you volunteered at the YMCA, Boys and Girls Club, recreation programs, community organizations, or at your church?

Some of the readily identifiable niches are:

- Gender
- Ethnicity
- Disability
- Employment, hobbies, activities
- Competitions, i.e., talent shows, art, dance, etc.
- Religious Affiliation
- Organizational Affiliation
- Community Groups
- Local Businesses
- Local Dollars for Scholars Chapter
- Local Financial Institutions
- Family Affiliation
- College-Career Goals
- Geographical Region
- Merit Qualification
- Service

# 65: get to know your counselor

Counselors deal with a lot of students, many of whom, are unfortunately, ungrateful. Become friends with your counselor and let him or her know that you want to apply for scholarships and that you appreciate any information that he or she can share with you. Once you get the information, do not be like the majority of students. Use it! If you successfully win a *scholarship*, go back to your counselor and personally let him or her know how much you won and how much you appreciate his or her help. Share your successes so that your counselor knows that you are a student who values his or her time and information. This sharing will help you to develop a relationship with your counselor and you will become more than a number.

# Chapter 13

## *Your Application Package*

Your application package represents the final steps in preparing for and getting accepted into the college of your choice. There is a scripture in the Holy Bible in the Book of Galatians [Chapter 6, verses 4-7]:

> *But let every man prove his own work, and then shall he have rejoicing in himself alone, and not in another. For every man shall bear his own burden ... for whatsoever a man soweth, that shall he also reap."*

As you put together your application package you will see what you have sown in the areas of:

- academics, standardized test scores, academic awards;
- extracurricular activities and community service;
- personal qualities; and

- intangibles.

What you have sown will determine the strength of your application package, which will influence the college admissions cycle that you choose to use. Some of the groups in which you may find yourself include:

- *Academic Superstar:* Your grades, course work, and standardized test scores have elevated you to the level of "Academic Superstar." You may have received a number of merit-based scholarships and find yourself a recruited student who has many college options. Hopefully, one or more of your options are schools that you have noted on your top-ten list.

- *Recruited-athlete:* Your success within one or more varsity sports has qualified you as a recruited-athlete. You may have already received offers via the National Letter of Intent program and now find yourself going through the difficult task of evaluating schools and offers. Hopefully, you have received scholarship offers from some of the schools on your top-ten list or are in a position to use offer letters from other schools to negotiate a financial-aid package with the schools on your list.

- *Strong Candidate:* The success that you have achieved within one or more of the areas (i.e., academics, extracurricular activities, etc.), makes you a strong candidate for admissions. While your acceptance is not guaranteed, you may feel that you are a strong enough candidate who is likely to receive enough acceptance letters that you will be able to compare financial-aid packages prior to committing to a particular college.

- *Legacy Student:* Regardless of whether you are an academic superstar, recruited-athlete, or strong candidate you have made up your mind and are committed to apply under the guidelines as a legacy applicant.

- *Weak Candidate:* After reviewing your application package, you realize that you are not a standout student in any area. However, if you are serious about going to college, then you, more than any other student, will have to do some research. Identify schools where you meet their minimum requirements, particularly schools with open admissions policies, and you must take the time to put together a quality application package and meet all of their posted deadlines. NO EXCEPTIONS!

# 66: decide when to apply

The admissions cycle that you choose to submit your application should reflect your situation, i.e., academic superstar, legacy student, weak candidate, etc. Sit down with your parents, mentor, or high school counselor to identify the admissions cycle that is best for you. Once you have made your decision, focus all your attention on creating quality application packages and meeting each college's posted deadlines.

**Early Decision:** This program is offered by approximately 270 colleges and is utilized by students who are absolutely certain of their first-choice school by the beginning of their senior year. Many colleges have higher admission rates for Early Decision applications.

**Early Decision II:** This program has the same restrictions as the Early Decision program. It is offered, by some schools, as a second round of Early Decision that has a later deadline than Early Decision (usually a January deadline).

**Early Action:** This program works like Early Decision, but is not binding and students are not obligated to attend the school if accepted. Students typically receive a response to their application ahead of regular decision applicants.

**Single-Choice Early Action:** This program works like a combination of Early Action and Early Decision. Like Early Action, students are not obligated to attend the school if accepted; however, like Early Decision, students may only apply to one school under the Early Action program.

**Regular Admissions:** The standard admissions evaluation cycle requires submission of your application by a deadline (usually in early to mid-January of the year in which you want to attend college). All applications received by the college are held until the deadline date and all applications are reviewed together. Late applications are reviewed AFTER the review of all applications received by the announced deadline.

**Rolling Admissions:** This evaluation cycle allows applications to be reviewed and decided upon as they arrive in the admissions office. It is best to get your application in as soon as possible after the announcement of the opening of the admissions cycle.

# 67: avoid common mistakes

Avoid such common mistakes as:

- contacting counselors too late to meet application deadlines;

- not filing your FAFSA in a timely manner;

- contacting the college admissions office so late that the majority of financial aid has already been committed to other students;

- failing to take the SAT I/ACT until the spring of your senior year;

- not filing for Early Admission to your first-choice school;

- not taking the required SAT IIs required by your first-choice schools; or

- submitting incomplete applications or financial-aid forms.

Keep a sharp lookout for these stumbling blocks:

- Submit the correct number of essays. If the directions state "choose one," select only one of the suggested essay topics.

- If the directions say to "complete all," write an essay for every topic requested.

- If an essay question has more than one section, provide an answer for every part. Make sure that your responses answer the questions—and make clear which response goes with which question.

- Compute the grade point average according to the instructions. Different schools use different methods for computing GPAs.

- Be careful not to confuse "country" with "county."

- Incorrectly listing the current year for your birthday (e.g. 1/1/03 instead of 1/1/88).

- Writing down the incorrect school name (e.g., Fisk instead of Spelman, or Yale instead of Amherst College).

- Using "white out." Do not undermine all your hard work because you were too busy, too anxious, too negligent, too sloppy, or simply too rushed to take the time to submit a complete, thorough, and quality application.

- Not following instructions

- Not clearly stating what you want to study

- Rushing

- Repeating yourself

- Burying outstanding accomplishments in mundane activities

- Writing down an incorrect home address

Incorrect word usage:

- *if* instead of *of*

- *an* instead of *and*

- *no* instead of *know*

- *from* instead of *form*

- *to* instead of *too*

- *though* instead of *through*

- *chose* instead of *choose*

- *whose* instead of *who's*

# 68: talk to your counselor

Different high schools have different policies and procedures regarding how they would like students to prepare their college application packages. Check with your counselor for the specific guidelines for your high school. Following is a checklist that would satisfy most high school counselors.

- ❑ Completed application (if you completed the Common Application, include any requested supplemental forms).

- ❑ Completed financial-aid application.

- ❑ Application fee (or fee waiver).

- ❑ Slides of your work, if your are an artist or photographer.

- ❑ CD or DVD, if your are an athlete, musician, dancer, or in theater.
- ❑ Résumé or listing of your activities.
- ❑ Student essay (if one is required).
- ❑ Teacher recommendations (or recommendation requests if required).
- ❑ Stamped, self-addressed postcard listing all enclosed materials for admissions to check off and return to you.
- ❑ Transcript request form (and appropriate fee).
- ❑ With the exception of the transcript request form and fee, enclose all your information in a large envelope with the correct postage (at least two first class stamps).
- ❑ Attach the transcript request and fee to the outside of the envelope.
- ❑ Take your information to your counselor.

Be aware of your deadlines and turn this package in to your counselor at least 3 weeks before it is due.

# 69: send thank you notes

Thank you notes should be sent to:

- admissions officers if you interview at a college

- people who write recommendation letters

- your high school counselor

- for each scholarship that you receive

# Chapter 14

## *Senior Year*

Your senior year will contain many important dates and deadlines. It is imperative that you organize yourself. You must know where your information is, you must keep track of important dates and deadlines, and stay focused. The first three years of high school have prepared you for and led you to this point. You should have performed your research, done your college visits, and prepared your essays. You should already have arranged your list of top-ten schools into numerical order. The only thing that should cause you to change your mind at this point is an offer package from a school that was not on your list—an offer that is so good that you must give the school and the package serious consideration.

# 70: don't quit

**What if you are not accepted into your first-choice school?**

The reality is, thousands of students will receive letters from their first-choice schools denying them admission. If you are one of these students then you will have to continue your planning. Do not allow a denial letter to discourage you from the pursuit of your dreams.

If you are committed to your first-choice school then become proactive and continue planning to be admitted through the school's transfer program.

1. Write a letter to the admissions officer to reiterate that the school is your first choice.

2. Ask the admissions officer about the school's transfer policy.

3. Accept admissions to one of the schools that you have been admitted to which has the type of school community, major, and classes comparable to your first-choice school.

4. Schedule your classes based on the transfer course requirements at your first-choice school.

5. Enter college and make a positive contribution to the school that you enter while you continue to prepare yourself to be admitted as a transfer-student to your first-choice school.

You may find yourself among those students who are not admitted into their first-choice college, but who discover themselves treasuring the experience at the college where they ultimately enroll.

# References

The content of the book has been taken entirely from the book, *A High School Plan for Students with College-Bound Dreams*. Please refer to the larger text for complete references. Refer to *A High School Plan for Students with College-Bound Dreams: Workbook*, for a comprehensive set of activities and worksheets to assist students with developing their high school plan and tracking their progress.

Wynn, Mychal. (2005). *A High School Plan for Students with College-Bound Dreams*. Marietta, GA: Rising Sun Publishing.

Wynn, Mychal. (2006). *A High School Plan for Students with College-Bound Dreams: Workbook*. Marietta, GA: Rising Sun Publishing.

For further information, visit our web site: www.rspublishing.

# Index